The GOOD OLD DAYS

by Caren B. Stelson

•

illustrated by
Christine Joy Pratt

Scott Foresman

Editorial Offices: Glenview, Illinois • New York, New York
Sales Offices: Reading, Massachusetts • Duluth, Georgia
Glenview, Illinois • Carrollton, Texas • Menlo Park, California

Some people call them "the good old days."

"The good old days" meant long days working on the farm. It meant early to bed and early to rise. It meant homemade bread and homemade toys. It meant quiet evenings with the family. Of course, it also meant no airplanes, no television, and no computers.

What would it be like growing up back then? Take a moment to find out. Say good-by to the "here and now." Say hello to "the good old days."

It's morning, but just barely. You've eaten
your breakfast of pancakes and fried potatoes.
Quick! It's time to get ready for school. You
comb your tangled hair and grab your tin lunch
pail. Then you head out the door.

It's November. There are only a few leaves
left on the trees. You like to go to school. It
gives you a break from all the chores you have
to do at home.

It's a long walk to school. Luckily, you get there just as Mr. Olson, the teacher, rings the bell. Both front doors are flung open. The boys make one line, youngest to oldest, in front of the left door. The girls make a line in front of the right door.

You find your place and squeeze in. Mr. Olson nods. Everyone files by, "making their manners" to him. The boys bow. The girls curtsy.

Inside, there is only one room. Boys sit on one side of the room. Girls sit on the other. The youngest are in the first rows. The oldest sit in back.

A big wood stove sits right in the middle. Firewood is flung beside it. Your desk is next to the window. Emily Swenson and Alice Johnson's desks are near the stove. They are the lucky ones. In the winter, you'll wish you had one of those seats.

Mr. Olson raps his desk with a stick.
Quickly you take out your slate and slate
pencil. You use slates instead of paper. Paper is
too expensive.

Suddenly Mr. Olson storms to the back of
the room where the oldest boys sit. He glares at
sixteen-year-old Joe Thompson.

"Use your right hand, young man," Mr.
Olson snaps.

Sheepishly, Joe Thompson shifts his slate
pencil from his left hand to his right. He knows
that writing left-handed is not allowed.

Reading lessons come first. Mr. Olson passes out the readers. The youngest get the easy ones. Yours is much harder.

Yesterday Mr. Olson suggested that you read the story, "Little John Learns to Tell the Truth." Almost every story ends with a lesson to learn.

The classroom is getting noisy now. It's so noisy you can hardly think. Some children recite poems out loud. Others shout arithmetic facts. One boy practices giving a speech. The younger children read to the teacher. No wonder some people call one-room schools "blab schools"!

Suddenly Emily Swenson screams. Then Alice Johnson wails. Out of the corner of your eye you see that a boy has tangled Emily's braid and tugged on Alice's hair.

Last week, Joe had flung his hat at the girls. Mr. Olson made Joe sit in the corner.

This is the first year Mr. Olson has taught in town. Miss Woods was the teacher during the summer. But some parents suggested they needed a stricter teacher.

All the families take turns having the teacher live with them. Next month Mr. Olson will be living with your family. How do you feel about that?

Mr. Olson says it's time for recess.
Everyone runs outside. Some girls play Cat's
Cradle with string. They try not to get it
tangled. Some boys play marbles. Some
explore the woods nearby.

Emily and Alice stay inside to bake potatoes
for lunch. They are sure to taste good. The
potatoes are picked from the school's garden.

After lunch, it's your turn to help with the school chores. You go out to the shed to get more wood for the stove. When you return, it's time for today's "spell-down." It's Friday. There's always a "spell-down" on Fridays.

The spell-down begins. But you catch a whiff of smoke. Quickly you look around. The room is filling up with smoke. Something is smoking inside the stove. Mr. Olson takes out a wet rag from the stove. It fell in somehow. Then he dismisses school. Everyone starts the weekend early.

This will make a good story for your family tonight. You practice telling it as you walk home. But you walk slowly. You know there will be many chores waiting for you.

What's that? Did you say you have had enough of "the good old days"? If you have, say good-by to them. Welcome back to the "here and now."

And don't forget to do your homework!